The

2024

CENTRAL
POETRY
PRIZE
AVENUE

EDITED BY BEAU ADLER

central
avenue

2024

Published by Central Avenue Poetry, an imprint of Central Avenue Marketing Ltd.
www.centralavenuepublishing.com

The poems 'Missed Calls and Heroin' and 'Hero's Death' appear in the book *The Music Was Just Getting Good*, reprinted with courtesy to Andrews McMeel Publishing

THE CENTRAL AVENUE POETRY PRIZE 2024

978-1-77168-366-1 (pbk)
978-1-77168-367-8 (ebk)

Published in Canada
Printed in United States of America

1. POETRY / Anthologies   2. POETRY / Subject & Themes - General

1 3 5 7 9 1 8 6 4 2

Keep up with Central Avenue

Dear Reader,

What you have in your hands is the answer to the very ambitious question: What if a small press like Central Avenue ran their own poetry prize?" When our publisher, Michelle Halket, pitched the idea to me in the summer of 2022, I thought we'd have a modest turnout. Enough submissions to make it work, but not so many that we'd have trouble drawing together a short list for the book. I had not, however, anticipated the sheer magnitude of our readership's interest in the contest, and I certainly hadn't considered how difficult a task it would be to select the ostensive "best" poems for our collection from the nigh-150 submissions we received. This task became especially difficult when I came to realize the masterful skill of everyone involved, from those who submitted, to those who were shortlisted, to those who won.

Poets are chemists of the heart. They are conjurers of vivid metaphors, maestros of eloquence, and architects of elaborate artistry. They are also generous. With but words alone, they invite us into their lives, into their own private worlds, and allow us to share in them together. It was my sincere pleasure to delve deep into the brilliant submissions we received, to be welcomed into your hearts and given the chance to stay a while.

I am grateful to everyone who made this book a tangible reality: to our tremendously talented poets, to the inimitable team at Central Avenue, and to the wonderful and supportive poetry community around us.

This is for you, and for all of us.

— Beau Adler, Editor

NOTES ON LOVING

YES

Say yes to swimming and wild blackberries
to hundreds of chickens grazing in the yard
to rolled down car windows and ukulele music
to the wind kissing your face

Say yes to joining a band, to singing in harmony
to remembering the old songs
Say yes to cauldron fire and purple bottles
filled with wildflowers

Say yes to film photography and giant looms
that take up too much space and too much time
Say yes to slowing down
to letting the nectarine juices drip down your chin
and onto the deck

Say yes to best friends and late-night laughter
yes to new places, new ideas, new awakenings

Say yes to saying no to the people who drain you
to the places that exhaust you
to the connections that wear you out to the studs

Say no until the only things left are unbearably
important to you, unspeakably important to the world,
and unendingly vital for your soul

ALIX KLINGENBERG is a poet, spiritual director, and creative dilettante. Alix lives near Boston, MA, with her family, two black cats, and a ridiculous dog named Cricket. She is queer and polyamorous, and has a passion for social justice, intersectional feminism, and the natural world.

I CANNOT THROW LOVE OUT THE WINDOW

Yes, Arthur Rimbaud you can
turn love into something small, press it, smash it, and toss it out the window
onto the highway at sixty miles per hour
just not in traffic
not in front of a cop.

Throw it down onto the floorboard, step on it, stomp it, kick it, break it
then throw it as hard as you can towards the west as the sun sets along
the back road on your way home.
Or save it, carry it into your house
spread love out
across the living room floor
light the corners with a lighter, watch it burn.

Laugh at it, spit on it, soak it in vinegar and drop it from the second story
window.
Write love right out of your body.
Sweat it out. Cut it out.
Put your finger down your throat, gag love out into the toilet
then flush —

After Rimbaud's line "I cannot throw love out the window." *Complete Works, Selected Letters,*
translated by Wallace Fowlie, The University of Chicago Press, 2005.

JJ CELLI is from the suburbs of Chicago, where she's active in the spoken word poetry
community. She also speaks on intimate partner violence in LGBTQI relationships. She is
working on her debut poetry series titled *Love Letters & Pocket Knives* as well as a memoir.

TO MY DEAREST

Hopefully one day you will read this message in a bottle
On paperback or on a card
I wake up with faith in the world, sometimes in God
Your love comes to me like a lightning rod
The cuts and bruises you've healed
The strength you've provided
The way you make me want to live

This world can be alarming but I'm happy
I can go out with confidence and be ready to rally
Scream and shout with the sun shining on my face
Knowing that one person will always love me for who I am
You make my heart race
We both thought we would never find our equal; we're an antiparallelogram

You make me feel at peace, an emotion foreign once before
Maybe there is a God out there; I will thank them for showing me angels do
exist
A sentence that I only wished
Once upon a starry night where stars were bright
And my hope was gone, replaced by fright
I love you and thank you for being my light

WILBER A. FLORES is a barista in New Jersey currently starting his journey as a writer. Outside of work, he likes to spend time eating and traveling with his fiancée, and honing his craft as a Coffee Master provided by a company with a little green mermaid on their cup.

TO MY YOUNGER BROTHERS

At not quite 1 and 5 years old
I wanted you to play and laugh

I tended your needs as best I could
while I hid a depression so rooted in my own childhood

it carved out my starving cheekbones
I tried to navigate door after door
and lost myself in the maze

I hope you feel my heart
hugging you through the screen

showing you a life you may not see
lived in front of you

I hope you learn the distance I hold
means you still have me around

I had to leave to keep myself
above ground

To my younger brothers
I hope you learn the doors you see in front of you

may not be the ones to choose
Sometimes the best ones are dust-covered

with a knock only you can hear

KELSEY BIGELOW is a poet from Des Moines, Iowa, and the author of *Sprig of Lilac* and *Depression Holders and Secret Keepers*. She's the founder and leader of the Des Moines Poetry Workshop, and a co-chair for the Iowa Poetry Association Poetry Slam.

MIMI'S INTERLUDE

i remember in my Mimi's sunroom
mornings in Lewisburg
white wicker basket-threaded chairs
a family of deer staring at us
and us peering at them.
i don't remember the smell in particular
other than it smelled like her
and what i can imagine would be
coffee in the morning, of course—
the kitchen was just steps away.
every time we would visit,
she'd greet us at the back with dreamsicle ice cream pops
and a trip to the movie store.
we'd wear out the same VHS films
like we had never seen Inspector Gadget before.
and in the morning,
it'd be cinnamon toast
dew on the grass
the sun tugging at daylight and
fawns looking to their mother.
i look back to see my Mimi
holding her coffee
smiling.
i'm perched in her chair
with gleaming admiration,
a visual conversation
of gentleness
only a grandmother and grandchild
can foster.

GRANT DAVIS is an artist and poet from Nashville, TN. He is currently based in Georgia, attending Savannah College of Art and Design. This is Grant's first official publication.

DECEMBER

December I still dream of you. Brisk air, stumbling through the woods. My head on your chest. The sun saying goodbye for good. Riding a bike like the days before I learnt how to drive. Waking up at 10am to your head resting on mine. *Do you want another coffee?* What I want is more time. Another month with you. Another Christmas, visiting the tree farms. Another moment sitting on your couch across from you. Brimming with tears. I'm just grateful to be here. *I'm grateful for you,* you said lying in your bed at 2am. A closing sentence on a beautifully turbulent year. I want another New Year's with you. Hearts ablaze. Arms wrapped around my body said, *I don't want to let you go.* Gazing out from the rooftop at the city. Your city. I told you, *I feel at home here.* But it wasn't the city lights that made me feel like I belonged. It was you. *Little lady,* you'd whisper. *You have nothing to worry about.* My mind had been read, but I couldn't shake the feeling. Two more days and I'd be back in my hometown. A million miles away from yours. Charlotte, a city. A place. A word. That meant wherever you are, *I'll meet you there.* My life-sized gateway to the best of me. That's what you became. What is six months after the time we spent together? I don't want another goodbye. *You're welcome anytime,* your mum said with tears in her eyes. *I can't speak or I'll cry,* I said to your brother. Holding on for dear life. Desperate to disappear in this home that had claimed my heart. *Ciao for now* you had said, when you kissed me goodbye. *Ciao for now* I whispered, as I boarded my flight.

AMELIA FAYE MICHELS is a multi-passionate Australian writer, poet, traveler, and the author of *You Are The Sun.* Through her poetry, she delves into the intricacies of love, capturing both the euphoria and the melancholy that accompanies deep connections.

THUNDERSTORM

I'm sitting here on my one-hundred-
and-something-year-old porch,
watching the late spring Louisiana
thunderstorm roll.
Watching the world whip
and bathe in the drumming
of the rain. All that
electricity dancing above.
It makes me smile from
ear to ear. It brings memories so warm
and bright and sloppy and
close I can almost taste
them.

Like the last August day at the farm where the
sunlight came through
the willow tree in the early mornings, before the
dew burned off, and you cried in the arms of your
heroes after learning to make heroes out of
those around you and the lightning came in
and the sky fell and pounded on the
greenhouse harder than we'd seen all summer,
and time seemed to stop, except to let the
flowers grow.

Like waking up from a nap at dusk, newly
twenty-one. Completely alone in this new land
I had brought myself to, made up of wild
rain and even
wilder people.

Or a year later, just after meeting the second
Big Great Love Of My Life, the one
with all the fire.
How, when it rained like this I used to
call him up.
He would answer, always, by asking *How are
you doing?* or *What are you doing?*
and I would say *It's raining.*
And he would be on his way.

LOTTIE SUMMERS is a poet, snake lover, and indomitable romantic from Olympia, WA. Her
work is spurred by themes of longing, proximity, heartache, and the cyclical nature of rot and
renewal taught to her by her agricultural upbringing. She currently lives in New Orleans.

MY RIBS ARE SOFT

Battered down by the
hands of those who wanted

my heart but didn't have
the patience to wait.

Every scar is a reminder
that the price of love

will always
be pain.

The shapes across my skin
show that no two people

ever break you the same.

But for you, I will gladly ache —
something deeper than
skin and bone.

May your love be the softest
ruin that I have ever
known.

LAUREN LEVI is a queer poet from Birmingham, England. Her work explores the highs of love, the lows of heartbreak, and the journey to mental health recovery.

BOMBSHELL BODY
after Kate Baer

Pillow talk body. I am not
a molded body, a Victoria's Secret
Angel body. This time, I'm the not-concerned-
what-men-want body. The missed-some-spots-
when-I-shaved body. You'll-be-begging-for-more-
when-I-strip-down-to-lingerie body.

Watch me redefine the bombshell body.
Revert it back to a warm body.
Shifting body. Ready for the changing seasons
body. Women were never meant to have
a static body,

IVA MARKICEVIC is a Serbian-American feminist poet. Her work has previously been published in Pile Press and the anthologies *Golden Arrows: Poetry of Goddesses* and *I DISSENT: An Anthology of Writing Women*: Presented by the Heartland Society of Women Writers.

THIS ISN'T EVEN MY FINAL FORM

i'm a masterclass in shapeshifting in that no two photos of me every really look the same, and self-love comes in the form of scrolling through my camera roll and finding the common thread that connects every single one of them. it's not about how i look, or what's happening in the moment, but rather looking for where you can see the real me breaking through. it's noticing where i had the courage to discard normalcy for authenticity in even the smallest bits. it's looking for that spark of confidence, no matter how dimly it may be glowing. it's watching that spark become a flame become a star become a galaxy with every passing year. it's realizing that i am the most me i've ever been in this very moment. and tomorrow, i will be the most me i've ever been in that moment. and ten years from now, i will be the most me i've ever been in that moment. and when my body is ash and my soul is stardust, i will be the most me i've ever been.

PARKER LEE [she/they]is a non-binary trans woman poet, as well as the author of *coffee days whiskey nights*. Parker resides in a coastal New Jersey town alongside wife and poetess amanda lovelace (and their three cats), where she can be found waxing autumnal every single day of the year.

BATS AND BIRDS

I was told I needed feathers to fly
so I spread out my wings and
glued each one to my sides
each day I'd prepare and leap toward the view
and each day I'd fall while the other birds flew

It wasn't until I let myself recognize
the feathers I bore were a weight in disguise
while they helped to lift others
they burdened my wings
I realized I'm different—
I screech while the other birds sing

So when asked why I strayed away
why I no longer pursue the light
I show off my wings, smile, and say
I'm much more myself at night

SARAH JANE PYPER is a poet and author of *STRAY*; a journey in, through, and out of faith. While writing has been a cathartic and healing experience for herself, she shares her poetry in hopes that it resonates with the reader to help them through their own experiences.

CICADAS

I lie waiting
for the heat of a summer
born only once
every 17 years

my feelings
tucked like wings
under the earth
of your memory

Will we have another summer?
Will we feel the heat again?

I do not dare make a move

I lie waiting
I lie waiting

Are you waiting too?

MICHELLE ARMITAGE is a mother and poet from Lake Country, BC. When not cuddled up with her kids, you will likely find her barefoot in the garden, trying new recipes in the kitchen, or capturing the magic of everyday life through words and photographs.

NOTES ON GRIEVING

WAYS TO GRIEVE

on the floor
in the bathroom
with shower water
steam
over the stove
in the kitchen
stirring the pot
petting a dog
in line
on the road
at a red light
by the bed
by the grave
at the theater
at the gas pump
in the drive-thru
in your sleep
with your coffee
in the mornings
together and
alone.

GRANT DAVIS is an artist and poet from Nashville, TN. He is currently based in Georgia, attending Savannah College of Art and Design. This is Grant's first official publication.

IF THE LEBANESE CIVIL WAR DID NOT FORCE MY FAMILY TO FLEE

If the bombs did not fall,
my mom would not duck at the memory
of fear thirty years later, when a harmless
helicopter flies overhead in a faraway land.

If the loud noise wasn't silencing,
maybe my mother would still have a voice.
My parents would still be in Lebanon, having never met,
my mother continuing her art career in Beirut,
not very far from where my father could've stayed in his family's house, instead of
leaving them behind in exchange for a college education in Ohio,
for money to be sent back, for hope to be held on to.

And maybe I would not have been born and maybe
I would've been okay with that,
if given the chance for my parents
to not have to evacuate, to never go back to their home,
to learn my home through them, the Arab-and-American-ness
of growing up as half and half but never complete.
My Arabic wouldn't be broken, it would be whole.

We would not be finding similarities in California's climate,
the mountains' silhouettes similar, the salty ocean air smelling identical,
the cedar trees just like our flag.
I wouldn't have to explain to people where my parents are from because they'd know.
I would know, too.

If the war did not conquer,
if my parents survived,
if they lived in Beirut for the last thirty years,
separately or together, would the explosion of 2020
have taken their lives? pushed them out? of a place they were never meant to be?

MAHA HASHWI is a poet and spoken word artist living in New York City. As a child of
immigrants, her work often details the experience of growing up Arab and Muslim in America. This
poem introduces an imagined future, or an alternative perspective to her family's life.

I WAS TOLD TO PRAY AND THE FATHER WOULD ANSWER

and yet this nursery of earth is still dark.

I am thinking about how an elephant can be kept in place by the same fraying rope that was used in its childhood. How a bind so small leaves its mark in the mind, renders the body defeated before it had even begun to fight.

There is something to be said about the delicate lives we live, how memories brand themselves as lessons into gray matter.

All this is to say I have said prayers in church a thousand times
and I still feel unheld.

I am thinking about how babies learn not to cry because
they realize no one is coming.
How such small bundles of newly-made body cannot survive
without touch, but

                    they learn not to ask.

ALYSSA PATIL is a writer based in Omaha, Nebraska. She writes fiction, essays, and poetry, unpacking ideas around religious trauma and the entanglement of mothers and daughters. Alyssa coaches a high school poetry club. She doesn't go to church anymore. Sundays are still holy.

BIT MY TONGUE A LITTLE TOO HARD

My heart is quaking, Ma – not breaking because I have inherited the set of
your shoulders. I want
to tear it out and hand it to you.

I want to show you, Ma, I want to tell you. But I don't.

I may have inherited my father's tinderbox temper, but from you I learned to
hold my tongue between my teeth.

Every time I bit my tongue my teeth sunk in deeper.
Deeper.
Deeper still until they met.

I didn't notice its absence for years, until one day you asked me why I loathed
you so. I looked down then (you had taught me to hold my tongue but never
to lower my gaze). A pink slug
writhed on the floor between us.

Mama, my heart is quaking and my hands are too. I want to tell you. Instead I
hold still under
your gaze and wait for you to look away. I glance at you then, the sun coming
through the
window making you a silhouette. The whole drive home we take turns.

I wanted to tell you then too; I wanted to tear out my heart and hand it to you
so you could see that yours and mine beat the same: I don't hate you, Ma, but I
cannot help that I have my father's
eyes.

MUSKAAN SINGH is a poet living in Pretoria, South Africa, and final year law student.
She feels strongly about mental health, and presented a TEDx Talk on the importance of
intersectionality for solutions in addressing mental illness.

LETTING GO OF THINGS THAT HURT TO HOLD

how did donkeyskin feel, dancing
in those dresses
her father had made
for her—

did she see
his smile in the silver,
white as the moon;
his waving hair
in the ripples of golden skirts;
his bright eyes
like a cloudless sky?

did she flinch
when the prince slipped
her lost ring, her
first engagement gift,
back onto
her finger?

I would have plucked the jewels
off the gowns
and pawned them;
burned the donkey's hide;
washed my skin with ashes
from another fire.

the fairy godmother will say
what she will
on the necessary things
that bring maidens
happily-ever-after:

we must hold on to
the magic gowns and capes
and missing rings
we find along the way—
but I would walk no more
with such reminders
of the story's wicked start.

RACHEL FINNEY is a poet from Springfield, Massachusetts, whose work has been published in
The Sigma Tau Delta Rectangle, Tiny Seed Literary Journal, Vocivia Magazine, and others.
She holds a BA in English literature from Westfield State University.

SHEDDING SKIN

In the dark of the living room my father sheds
his skin again. I hear grating, the sound
promising yet another renewal (but I know

better—a serpent, too, has one final layer,
it has to). As I turn to look at him,
he pauses, takes a seat in front of

the TV. His face smudged on my retina.
His oak-brown eyes cutting through
the fuzz on the screen hissing in its own

language. I ask, how many more. He
won't speak. Passing car lights pull his shadow
by its ear, stare clogged with memories. He won't

speak. His arm, stretched out as if reaching
through a portal, holding the remote.
Corroded batteries leaking. Taped to not fall apart,

he switches channels back and forth.
The rubber button click, click, click.
From white noise to white noise to white noise.

KONSTANTINOS PATRINOS is a writer based in Berlin, Germany. His work has appeared
in *RHINO Poetry, Hunger Mountain Review, Rust + Moth, Toyon, Clackamas Literary Review,
Pinyon*, and others. He is a high school teacher of political science and philosophy.

MARY, PT. 2

The 16-year-old Mary sits in the driver's seat,
one holy hand at midnight on the steering wheel,
scrolling on her phone in the other.
She picks a song, turns up the volume.
She's probably not wearing makeup,
her unwashed hair gathered back in a ponytail.
Maybe she's wearing Joseph's oversized hoodie.
Maybe she's picking up the son of God from daycare.
Maybe Mary likes Taylor Swift. Maybe the newest album is playing.
She's never been the type to scream song lyrics in the car before
and God knows she's never been the selfish type,
never will be in the days to come.
But for a song's length, her fist keeps time on the wheel
as the queen of heaven sings, as the teen mom grieves:
My girlhood my girlhood my girlhood

ALYSSA PATIL is a writer based in Omaha, Nebraska. She writes fiction, essays, and poetry, unpacking ideas around religious trauma and the entanglement of mothers and daughters. Alyssa coaches a high school poetry club. She doesn't go to church anymore. Sundays are still holy.

PREVENTATIVE MEASURES

i could never eat as fast as my food could rot
milk sours
mold blooms on bread
even the oreos go stale
i stand each week at the counter
separating the good from the bad
the salvageable from the unsalvageable
using my knife to cut around and through
i wonder what would happen if
i carved away the damaged parts from myself
a slice off the top here
halved there
skinned
chopped
piece by piece
i could dispose of the bad bits
cut away the disease before it has a chance to spread
i stand at the counter
the knife in my hand debating
how much would be left
how much could i get away with
maybe this could be considered
preventative measures
i put the knife down

ALYSSA STEIN is a poet based in Maryland. Stein is a two-time Hodgkin's lymphoma survivor
and has had her work appear in *Elephants and Tea* magazine. She spends her free time reading,
writing, and spending time with her husband and dogs.

HERO'S DEATH

Addiction descended upon our home—
entered right through the front door.
An act of asymmetric warfare—
on the longest day of the year.
Took you as prisoner.
I never saw you again.

But I know,
I know that you gave it your all
even on the days you lost.
And I know,
I know you prayed to live
even on the days you begged to die.
And I know,
I know that you didn't mean
half the unfortunate things you screamed.

I know you were scared. So were we.

A war-torn family never returns to who they used to be.
Battle scarred, visiting the graveyard,
collecting sympathy cards.

Whoever claims addiction only targets the weak
never met your courageous spirit,
never felt your brave heart beat.
Whoever claims you had this coming
never had to sing *happy birthday*
to an empty chair as the candle burns.

You fought like hell.
I promise, in all my retellings,
you die a hero's death.

ALICIA COOK is a multi-award-winning writer and mental health and addiction awareness advocate from New Jersey. Her writing often focuses on addiction, mental health, and grief. She has released four poetry collections, including the bestselling *Sorry I Haven't Texted You Back*.

YOU NEVER SOFTENED

They warned me about your nature. How
someone punched a hole in your nurture,
discarded it in the trash, like you do—with people.
They called you the devil—I wouldn't agree,
if that was true, that meant the devil's
in me.

I walked with years trailing stars, burning
out wishes of a child's longing
to meet her father. Maybe I needed
your love to stitch up my abandonment.

I set out to find you, only to learn, they were right.
Your edged tongue rang into the phone,
you told me not to bother "your family."
How I folded like a paper napkin
and cried, "but I'm your
family too."

It wasn't long after, February's cold
arrived with my sister's death. You flew
up for the funeral. Irony and time placed us
all in the same room. One daughter in a casket
and one a flattened wallflower.
Both dead to you.

Somehow I knew it would be my only
chance to meet you. I walked into my fear,
cupping my rejected heartbeat in hand,
as I opened mine to yours. I counted all 20
seconds my palm waited, suspended
in air. You never said a word
and walked away—an image
permanently pressed.

That was the closest I ever was to
you. My stubbornness dreamed one
day you would soften, make it right.

You died, more stubborn than I.

JEN HOLLY is a Canadian poet who writes about love, loss, and healing, sharing vulnerable
pieces on social media. Jen Holly released her first poetry collection, *All Is Fair in Love Poems*, in
2022. She has a Master of Social Work, and a BA in psychology, and works in social work.

LET ME BE HONEST

once you have a dead baby,
you can't help yourself. you just
keep planning for the next
worst thing, because now
you know — nothing
is too sacred to be lost. so
you hold your breath
for one year, ten years,
a lifetime of lifetimes, and then
somehow, even after all that,
after tiptoeing the earth to escape
calamity's notice, it manages
to find you anyway: cancer,
death, heart failure, an accident,
an innocent slip into a devastating
fall. and you thought you were
ready, that you'd always be ready,
from that day that turned
you inside out so your tender
guts hung on display as you held
on to that dead baby for dear
life — you'd thought that you
and grief were old friends now,
that he could never surprise
or scar you again, or at least
not nearly so badly, surely not.
but now your tears tell the truth:
that you're never ready
no matter how much you've lost,
you're never ready
and never okay,

not even a little,
not even after so much practice,
when it happens
again

ELIZABETH WILDER is the author of several poetry collections, including *I Promise I Tried,* as well as a novel and a guide to writing poetry. In addition to her quirky family and their too-many pets, Elizabeth is in love with moon-gazing, dancing wild, and drinking too much coffee.

TO MY CHILD THAT COULD HAVE BEEN

I apologize
little lime,
for you
did not deserve
the fate of a
relinquished existence.

It was not
easy when
your future
was pitted
against mine.

You, swirl of cells
offered more
comfort than
I will concede.

The hushed conversations
we shared
veiled by berating
droplets beating
into my spine
remain in sanctum
my friend.

I understand
a mother must
love her child
and
I failed
at doting your
unabridged
form enough
to save you.

Your undoing
was a means of
protection from
a world I was
in no position
to offer you.

If we had left this world
in tandem
I would be content
with singing you
embalmed lullabies.

The brokenness
from the womb
curdled a draining soul.

When you ponder
your being, I pray
you forgive me for
choosing an end
over a tender existence.

ANNA KUSHNER is a bit of a globetrotter — originally from Michigan, she currently lives in Sydney, Australia, where she works in marketing. She graduated from Michigan State University in 2022, where she studied international relations and poetry. This is her first published piece.

GRIEF, OR THE POTENTIAL OF GRIEF

sits heavy in the middle of your stomach
a chafing mass of concrete and
eighteen years of memories

it scrapes against your intestines and draws blood
presses up against reserves of happiness
tucked away in the pocket of your hipbone

here, let me lay my hand above your lungs
where air is stubborn and shifting
and feel the pulses of that horrid thing you call a

heart, still beating. if i could i'd crawl down
your throat with cotton fingers and clean
the running lines of red and salt.

carve off the rough stone edges and force it
to smallness; i'd stop the shards from
seeping into your bloodstream, but i can't.

so let me lay my hand above your lungs
where the air is stubborn and shifting
and feel the pulses of that wonderful thing you call a

heart.

GITIKA SANJAY is a poet and writer from San Jose, California. Gitika has been published in *Sunday Morning at the River's Folly Took a Seat and Laughed in Our Faces*. She is also the author of *Queer Folk in Strange Times*. She is an avid lover of tea, piano, and extended metaphor.

TAKE ME OUT OF MY SKIN

imagine this:
a separation running
down a mirror—a fault-line;
San Andreas in the corner of
my eye. i'm forced outside of the
glass. imagine that my mind is alliteration,
that it tumbles over itself like feet tripping over
uneven stones. it falls to the ground outside of the glass.
its arms searching for purchase in the empty air.
it is something made, which means it is
something that is false. so that you
can imagine this: a hole in the
reflection with another pair
of eyes staring
back.

GITIKA SANJAY is a poet and writer from San Jose, California. Gitika has been published in *Sunday Morning at the River's Folly Took a Seat and Laughed in Our Faces*. She is also the author of *Queer Folk in Strange Times*. She is an avid lover of tea, piano, and extended metaphor.

SCARS

She called to me.
I found her
soaking in the tub,
her jet-black wig off,
exposing her
porcelain white scalp.

Delicate bubbles
made a thin veil
over her frail frame.
She had hoped they
would hide her scars,
but they didn't.

I scanned the room
searching for clues,
too afraid to speak
or to look directly
at her vulnerability.

Eventually my eyes
landed on her
missing breasts and
the red, raised incision
that had cut her in two—
armpit to armpit.

She was sewn back together
with black thread.
"Mama!" I gasped.
She slowly turned
her head away
as the bath water
began to quake.

AMY LEVITIN GRAVER (she/her) is a writer, poet, artist, mother, photographer, baker, and designer from Connecticut. She serves on the Board of the Connecticut Poetry Society and is a member of the Blackstone Library's poetry group and is writing her first collection of poetry.

ORAL TRADITION

We all remember it a little differently—
I call my cousin four years later
and we tell each other
the moments we forgot.

She sends me a photo of myself,
with greasy hair and sweatpants,
grinning over a plate
of pork chops—
the first real meal
either of us had eaten
in weeks.
But I can only recall bags and bags
of Burger King
eaten family style
around the hospital bed.

I tell her about the time
I saw her crying in the hallway
as I entered the nursing home;
how she fooled me
into thinking
he was already dead.
For her, it had been
a step away from the crowd,
a moment to breathe different air,
one of many.
We laugh about that story together, now.

I am learning—
an epic poem sounds different
in every singer's mouth.
We focused on different features
when we first heard the tale.

Now, we sing the structure,
the rhymes and epithets,
but rewrite the lines between
without ever realizing.

I think about my mother,
my grandmother,
my uncle,
my brother—
the whole of us,
everyone who waited for a man to die
in that room
at the end of the hall.

I wonder what poems
the rest of them could write.

RACHEL FINNEY is a poet from Springfield, Massachusetts. Her work has been published in *The Sigma Tau Delta Rectangle, Tiny Seed Literary Journal, Vocivia Magazine*, and others. Rachel holds a BA in English literature and served on the campus literary journal as editor-in-chief.

MISS YOU. WOULD LIKE TO SIT ON THE COUCH WITH YOU.
after Gabrielle Calvocoressi

Do not care if you don't bring your voice box. Or if you want to ask the same question forty times. Would want nothing more than to sit on the couch with you. Miss you. Know how hard it was to speak in the end. Don't need more than to sit with you. Wish we could share cream-filled bonbons and chocolate espresso beans. Would bring out all your favorites. If you could just come back. Wouldn't even need to stay that long. Just enough for some carefully wrapped cabbage rolls and fingerling potatoes. The gravy like a soup. Cook for you the way you would for me. We could leave the fragmented memories on the plates. Miss you. Miss you telling me to never be alone. Your red puffer jacket. The sound of your loafers on hardwood floor. Miss your laugh, your hair-curlers, your big, warm hands. They felt so small during the worst of it. See the blue all over me? See how lonesome I am? Know I wanted you to go. Watching you suffer for so long was like circling the drain for years. I couldn't take more of the spinning. Wish you had stayed anyway. Wish you would come through the door and scoop me up like I was still five years old. We could hide sweets under your pillowcase. Take a drive to Talbots. Buy you all the sweater sets you wanted. Miss you. Wish I could feel you near me. Wish I had some sign, anything, really, that you're okay and with us still. Write me a letter with your ghost hands. Call me on your ghost phone. You left me here with so many things to tell you. So much I need you to tell me, still.
Miss you. Been waiting by the door. Teacups ready and everything. Hand outstretched to lead you in. The last time we spoke I could hear it in your voice. You were dying so slowly for so long I sometimes forgot the ending. That there would be one. Know you had to go. Wish you didn't. I cry so easily now. I am an open wound that you can press into. My sides like buttons. And the tears consume me. Know you wouldn't like that. I'd tell you it's just unexpressed love. Everything I have to give you that I can't. That the time we have is never enough.
Truth is, I never wanted to be named after you. Was so afraid of how lonesome our name would sound when it was just me left. Turns out, I was right. Miss you. Wish you could come back and be you and I could be me.

KIRA SANTANA (she/her) lives on the island of O'ahu, where she is a graduate student, poet, and hula dancer. Her work is influenced by experiences with chronic illness, grief and healing, and her childhood growing up in Norway. She received the Myrle Clark Award for Creative Writing.

THE KEEPER OF LOST TIME

I like to think
that lost time isn't really lost,
that it waits someplace
else for us.

in a small house upon a hill,
maybe, with jasmine covering the porch
and sunrise pooling through the
windows like honey;

plums and mislaid days ripening
on the old oak counters,

sunflowers in mason jars
and coffee that never gets cold.

I like to think
I'll find you there,

at the end of both our days.

HARRIET SELINA is a queer writer and tutor from Sussex, UK. She has a degree in English literature and an MA in modern and contemporary literature. Her poetry explores the crevasses and contours of trauma recovery, grief, and connection.

NOTES ON CREATING

IF I WERE A BETTER POET,
I WOULD REMEMBER

If I were a better poet, I would remember
the day my partner taught me how to boil eggs.
I would be able to describe the way the curtains
moved in the breeze of the open window,
how the clouds were fading across the horizon
after a morning rain. I would remember
the day of the week. (At least I would pretend
to know these things.) The easy metaphor here
is the breaking of the shell (my shell)
the simple shame (my shame)
is not having known how to do this before.
However, the truth I can tell you:
it is a Tuesday when I am writing this,
the sun is shining, there are no clouds,
and I decided to boil an egg with my lunch.
Beyond that, I can tell you the cracking
of a boiled egg, the shell crumbling against
my fingertips, requires a sort of fierce gentleness
and patience I did not have and might not have,
if it weren't for the hands that taught me.

ABBY BLAND (she/they) is a Kansas City writer and performer whose work has appeared in
Ghost City Review, What Are Birds? and elsewhere. Her debut chapbook, *The Odds Against a
Starry Cosmos,* was published with Perennial Press.

OUROBOROS

Crown my head as Medusa
My intrusive thoughts a Hydra
Cut one down, two more take its place
Cut one down, cut one down, cut one down

My mind is full of writhing and rattling
Snake oil, snake venom
The difference between poison and medicine
Is how much you can swallow

Time moves like a snake
All S-curves and undulations
My days move like tides
Ebb and swell, peak and depression

Eat of myself, tail down my throat
Consume my own ending
Eternity is a mouth full of blood that says
"Soon my skin will shed and I will no longer be
A thing you have touched."

C.J. COLLIGAN is from Long Island, New York, and is a graduate of SUNY Binghamton with a Master's in elementary education. C.J. has been writing poetry for as long as they can remember, and this is their first published poem. They teach children with special needs.

THERE'S A WORD FOR THAT

I've been having trouble writing lately.
And it's not that I can't find the words,
it feels like they have left me completely.
No, this isn't writer's block.
This . . . is abandonment.

So I decided to start reading about words,
and I learned so many things.
For example: *Nefelibata,*
a Portuguese word meaning "cloud-walker."
One who lives with their head in the clouds
and doesn't bend or mold their creativity
to what society deems acceptable.

Or *amphigory.*
An English word for a piece of writing
that appears to have meaning
but is just nonsense.
I've got notebooks full of amphigory.

I learned that the sickness which lives
in the pit of my stomach
and at the back of my throat
and under my tongue
when I become a nervous wreck
is called *collywobbles.*

And did you know there is a word
for a knife fight?
It's *snickersnee.*
And *callipygian* is when one possesses
beautiful and shapely buttocks.

I even found words for some of my favorite things.
Grimalkin is a 16th-century word for cat.
Komorebi is the Japanese word
for rays of sunlight that spill through the trees.
And *Yugen* is a deep, emotional response
to the universe.
I feel it every time I look at the stars.
But then I came across the word *lacuna*.
A blank space.
A missing part.
And your face flashed into view.
Turns out I wasn't missing words,
what I was really missing was you.
I have yet to come across a word
for this type of grief.
Maybe, there just isn't one.

JILLIAN CALAHAN (she/they) is a poet and short story writer from the Pacific Northwest. If she's not writing, she's probably lost in a bookstore somewhere. Along with books, she enjoys crafting, puzzles, a good cup of tea, a pretty sunset, and spending time with her 3 cats and 2 dogs.

TREATMENT PLAN

The poet diagnosis is yes,
Incurable, but not the killer
You first claimed it to be.

You are deemed, not doomed,
An eligible curator of madness.
Watch as you blend ecstasy
And terrible torture onto a lined canvas.
Is that not art too?

You were never writing wills,
But decrees of immortality.

And you learned we are all always fleeting
Which is why the little shrike bird
Deserves his own spotlight.

The lines that came so easily from your mind scarred,
So you find it's much more enriching
To seek stanzas in the perseverance of mornings,
And not, as you thought,
As draining or dull to find new scripture to write
When you indulge yourself in the process of recovery.
To stitch yourself together with each delicate stanza.

So the poetry you want to be
Is not waiting under the covers of common hiding places,
But on the cusp of each evening.

Where the sky and sea meet,
Where I am standing, breathing,
Listening. And you,
On the other side of this day,
Are on your way to me.

FRANCES ISLER is a student at the University of California, Santa Barbara, where they study
English with a specialization in creative writing. They have been published in the *Colonial Heights
Newsletter*, in their university literary journal, and with the America Library of Poetry.

AUTOPSY OF A POET

The hole in her body
was made by a 9 mm Glock,

but really it was there
for much longer. And if the words
couldn't fill it, maybe a bullet could.

A scalpel to her skin showed
her blood was as thick as ink
even though it no longer pulsed
through her veins with the fervor
of someone perpetually thinking
the unthinkable, imagining the
unimaginable, and explaining
the unexplainable.

Her spine was bound with pages—
processes so sharp, the coroner
would easily get paper cuts
if he wasn't careful while sliding
back her skin and watching
the untold verses crawling out
of her, like spiders desiring
to make a permanent residence
in the world, however futile.

Her tongue still held traces
of similes, hyperboles, mysteries
that lingered on her taste buds,
a flavor that nothing
could erase. Words
used to spill out from

her lips, hesitant but
sharp, like her tongue
was holding Chekhov's
gun and maybe that's why
she pulled the trigger.

LEXI MERRING is a master's student at Montclair State University and a graduate of Fairleigh
Dickinson University with a BA in creative writing and psychology. She has been published in
Sigma Tau Delta Rectangle, Women Who Write's Goldfinch, and *The USA Boxing News*.

THIS IS NOT A SLAM POEM

it's a fall
asleep, shut the door
quiet so you don't wake up poem

it's not a hefty boots
up the steps, stumble
to the stage poem
it's a pen
under a soft hand
dance
    across
        the
           page
              poem

not a nervous laugh,
crisp voice, feedback
from the mic poem
but a scribble,
whisper, sing-song,
glad you're in my life poem

not a rustle in
the crowd or applause
from out of town poem
it's a thumbs up, or
a smile. it's a
simple settle down poem

it's not a heavy heart,
hidden meaning, hope
that you catch on poem
it's a thanks
      for staying
      with me after
      everybody's gone home

SARAH NANNINI is a young poet from California. She won the 2023 Elliot Ruchowitz-Roberts Monterey County High School Poetry Award. She strives to use her passion to express herself while helping others find their voice.

DORA MAAR

after Pablo Picasso's Weeping Woman

Oh Dora, he has peeled the olive skin
off your face, ripped your flesh away
down to your cheekbone, grayed

it with grief that was never yours,
oil-painted his misery into your tears,
darkened the crease of your brows,

dyed your clothes for mourning,
and beat each purpling bruise
underneath your eyes.

All portraits of me are lies.
They're Picassos.
Not one is Dora Maar.

Sweet enigmatic woman, uncredited muse,
his gaze will never capture you.
These jagged lines framing your face

like shards of glass cannot taint your name,
your way with film; they will not erase
the visions you had for a photograph.

SAAKSHI PATEL was born and raised in Bombay. She earned an MA in poetry from Queen's University Belfast. She got her BA in English literature and language from the University of British Columbia. Saakshi currently teaches English in Vancouver.

THE CREATION OF LANGUAGE

If we did not have language,
I would create the word "light"
from the fire in your eyes
and the word "home"
from the warmth of your thighs
and the word "strength"
from the jut of your chin
and the word "taste"
from the sweet salt of your skin.

I would create the word "water"
from the wet of your lips
and the word "dance"
from the curve of your hips
and the word "time"
from the scars on your wrists
and the word "survive"
from the strength of your fists.

But I would not create a word for "love."
We would live that, instead.

ELISON ALCOVENDAZ'S work has appeared in *The Rumpus, Rattle, Santa Monica Review, The Portland Review, Under the Gum Tree,* and others. He has an MA in creative writing, and his short fiction was selected as a Best Small Fictions 2020 winner. He lives in Sacramento, CA.

IF YOU SEE MY WORDS DRIFTING YOUR WAY

If you see my words drifting your way
Reach out for them and let them stay
They have travelled so much and travelled so far
They carry songs of life
The dark and light
And all the things they have seen in between
I pray they bring you a little warmth and some comfort
Like they brought me on my foggiest days
I hope you keep them close to your heart
And when you release them
Allow them to take a little bit of you with them —
Just a tiny part

SHEFALI DANG is a Toronto poet who discovered her love for words in high school. She enjoys
reading and immersing herself between the pages of a good book. She also enjoys photography,
cooking, and trying out new recipes. She also enjoys photography, traveling, and cooking.

NOTES ON LIVING

THE MEANING
OF LIFE IS
LOCKED UP IN AN OLD
LIBRARY SOMEWHERE
BURIED DEEP BELOW
PILLARS OF HISTORY
AND COVERED UP BY
DUST AND WAR,
SOMEWHERE SO LOW
WE CAN'T RECALL
WHERE IT IS ANYMORE.

APRIL HILL WRITING started as a means of escape from thoughts that caused anxiety and confusion. There is an underlying weirdness people do not always feel a fondness for, through scattered thoughts and questions we can connect people and things, to feel a little bit better.

OPEN THIS WHEN YOU NEED ME MOST

after Ocean Vuong

Open this when you need me most, even if it's every day.

Open this when I'm well into the next day's morning and you're still trying to get through the previous day's night.

Open this when you're feeling lonely and you're tired of telling me something we cannot change.

Sweet love of mine,

I wish I had hands that could stretch 4000 miles, just so I could hold you. I would learn magic if it brought you to me. I would learn how to pray one more time if God would listen to me again after I abandoned him at 16.

But in the loneliness of this night, when there's nothing I can do to change the way your heart aches without reason, close your eyes and picture me. Picture me with my arms wrapped around you and my chin on your head, you can rest your ear on my chest and fall asleep to the sound of my heartbeat.

Picture me fast asleep right next to you, dreaming of you so I never have to spend a second of my life not memorizing your face.

Picture me kissing your hands. Picture me running my fingers through your hair. Picture me in love. Picture me picturing you to get through the day because it's the only thing that gets me through not being with you.

And when all else fails, wake me up in the middle of the night to tell me something I will never get tired of hearing. Tell me you need me, say you

miss me, let grief leave through your eyes and I will stay with you through it because I'd rather be talking to you than sleeping.

You can tell me just how long a human can go without sleep before their body gives out, and I'll break the record if it means you'll spend one less night with heaviness drowning you from the inside.

Open this when you need me most, even if it's every day.

Open this when I'm well into the next day's morning and you're still trying to get through the previous day's night.

Open this when you're feeling lonely and you're tired of telling me something we cannot change.

God, please just open this till I find a way to bring myself to you.

RIDA AAMINA is a queer Indian poet born in UAE. She writes passionately about queerness, mental illness, and relationships with people, food, and God, but most importantly, the world through the eyes of a young woman struggling to find her place.

CHRONIC ILLNESS TAKES NO DAYS OFF

eastward
like sunlight
the light filters
in through the open
window & i stand
by the kitchen counter peeling
an orange
the morning rolls
in like a swollen
wave & i am still trying
i take my meds
with my own
fingers clasping
curling
letting
go & welcome
the new day
like fresh rainfall
syrah lips & an inner
calm returning
to my ribcage
some
days it feels like
the universe eats
my heart like a pomegranate
and all i can do is
watch but in between
surviving
there is so much
living
so i turn
my head to
the light
bathe in the peach sunrise
while my jaw
sits in my face
like a landslide

about to
happen my stomach
like smashed up
rocks
i know i am
sick
have been
for a while
but i no longer
want what i can't
have
instead i am
so proud of
how my body is
existing
in the midst of
so much grief
there is still
all this
joy
here & i
have so
many dreams constantly
playing
i run the tap
to fill my cup
water
splashing
or is it spluttering?
anyway it flows
i hold the cool
glass & think of quiet
winter days &
blankets that smell
like home
open the refrigerator
& a city falls
out
somewhere i maybe
change
my name rent an

apartment over a
flower shop
spend hazy afternoons
reading in parks walking
along rows of tulips
tell people i'm happy
for the hell
of it
check my blood
work & only
see the improvements
dance when i feel
like weeping
curl into
a book & be
someone else
get lost between
the pages
then come home
to myself
i will slowly
get better
i have to believe
i will & until
then i will walk my
dog eat on
time forgive
my body focus on
this quiet joy & all my
delicate
dreams call
my doctor
listen
to music braid my
hair embrace
the mess &
live.

KIRA SANTANA (she/her) lives on the island of O'ahu, where she is a graduate student, poet, and hula dancer. Her work is influenced by experiences with chronic illness, grief and healing, and her childhood growing up in Norway. She received the Myrle Clark Award for Creative Writing.

LUNATIC

RUNNER-UP
THE CENTRAL AVENUE
POETRY PRIZE
2024

I think the moon is a little bitch,
incessant and itching for earthly attention,
cute and round and gray but aloof,
just like the neighbor's cat.
The dusty lunatic emerges tonight,
robed in tarnishing silver, familiar
with a touch of Cheshire drama:
sitting silent, directing our chaos.
She merely does a quick half-spin
to churn the seven humble waters,
and shows herself once in quarter capacity,
sparking mayhem for humankind.
A moody moon, she shies away,
invisibility-cloaked. Enrage her
with space trash or visits unannounced,
she will flash in ominous red.
I think our precious flaky moon
curses planetary centripetal ties
and desires to break away.
Experienced in serial manipulation,
she craves free space and edges
two inches out of orbit each year.

SAAKSHI PATEL was born and raised in Bombay. She earned an MA in poetry from Queen's
University Belfast. She got her BA in English literature and language from the University of
British Columbia. Saakshi currently teaches English in Vancouver.

GROWING UP WITH A DISABILITY IS VERY CONFUSING

On one hand, you are taught that
the world is not going to understand you
and might be scared of you.
On the other hand...
Well, I don't really have another hand.

From a very young age I held a dichotomy in my mind.
Be independent and do everything you can to be normal...
But also be comfortable with who you are.

At 26 weeks and 2 pounds,
I was born into the palm of my father's hand.
My own hand the size of his thumbprint.
The doctor's nickname for me was miracle,
but he charted it spastic
cerebral palsy.
If I survived the year my
nickname would be
lucky.

I survived a whole lot more.
I survived strangers assuming
I couldn't speak, read, or write.
I survived more than your average
schoolyard bully.
I survived sideways glances
and muffled laughter of things
they'll never understand.

My left arm is weak,
muscles are tight and unforgiving.
My right arm flexes with fourfold the strength.
A strange dichotomy splitting my body in two.

But who am I?
I'm unpredictable bone aches,
and waves of fatigue.
I'm endless calculations
of stamina and balance.
I'm a scared, tired little kid
just begging for someone to hold my hand.

How can I tell the world who I am
when every morning I wake up
feeling like the world outside
is a boxing ring and
I have to put on gloves
just to leave the house?

See, the bell rang.
The next match is beginning
and it's me against the world.
I might as well punch back,
and I've got one hell of a right hook.

SAMUEL FAULK lives in Yakima, WA, and is the author of *The Devil's Thesaurus*. He is a
librarian with an English and teaching background who views the written word as fuel for the
soul. In his spare time he watches way too many shows and enjoys writing fiction/poetry.

MISSED CALLS AND HEROIN

By the third missed call,
I'm convinced you're dead.

Hopefully warm in your bed
or in your car with your favorite song playing.

Dead anywhere but
the Rite Aid bathroom—
surrounded by strangers
more inconvenienced than heartbroken
upon finding your body.

Dying is a private pilgrimage.
　　　The nerve of you to carry it out in a public space—
one I need to pass on a regular basis.

I'm forced to go about my day
Like you're not dead.
　　　How dare you.

Post office.
Pens are out of ink and the line is too long.
Plus, you're dead.

Gas station.
Attendant tells me I'd be prettier if I smiled.
Plus, you're dead.

I drive off. Doing the math—
14 hours since last contact.
There's no saving you by now.
You're cold. Probably blue.
Morticians have makeup that could help with that.

What was your last thought?
Did you think of me?
You're my only thought these days.
I heard it's just like falling asleep.
Does that mean you'll still get to dream?

Tell me you at least had ID on you.
Make that part easy on us, please.
Because the rest of our lives are going to be so hard.

The truck in front of me kicks up something.
The starburst the rock creates in my windshield
mimics the shape and sparkle of my earrings I know you love.
You told me when you weren't dead.

I begin to bargain.

If you're not dead,
I'll give you the earrings.
　　　Even if you sell them.
　　　Even if you die in them next week.

At least we'll have another week.

27 is such a cliché age to make an exit.
Just wait another month—
be an individual and die at 28 instead.
I swear I—abruptly
　　　my phone buzzes.

It's you.
You're not dead.

ALICIA COOK is a multi-award-winning writer and mental health and addiction awareness advocate from New Jersey. Her writing often focuses on addiction, mental health, and grief. She has released four poetry collections, including the bestselling *Sorry I Haven't Texted You Back*.

MY FATHER'S ACCENT

My father's accent is enough
to make you wrinkle your nose in disgust
but you have never had to balance
a second language on your tongue
        and even if you think you could
remember that my mother tongue makes sounds
that leave English at a loss for letters

HARMAN KAUR is a writer and the author of *Phulkari*. She was born and raised in British Columbia, Canada, and now lives in the Bay Area, California. Harman is a Panjabi Sikh woman who uses her writing to express and explore the complexities of her identity.

PLEASE

limited since the 18th year.
to exist as a more than half,
is still less than full.

can a soul be filled
with
deficit language?

i'd do
anything
to redefine
loveloss.
kept waiting—the approaching spill—
please.
this vessel
can take
in excess.
this vessel
can be more than full.

i'll let the rim runneth over it all.

TYLER AUSTIN is a National Youth Theatre member and has performed at the SoHo Theatre, Stratford Theatre Royal, Royal Court Theatre, and the Arcola Theatre. Tyler has a background in law and has worked with the University of London Group and York.

LIKE A TREE THAT LOSES ITS LEAVES

like a tree that loses its leaves
in the dead of winter
i, too, grow tired
of my own permanent nature

as another year passes
holding on to nostalgic branches
reminds me just how temporary
both every ray of sun
and every dark cloud
that vegetates me
lasts

and with my deadened limbs
i spread my arms wide open
for every sprouting root
tangled with the past
as all that has buried me
has planted me a new bed of seeds

and with every changing season
i get another chance
to shed the weight of who i once was
off the layers of my back

CHRISTINE MARIE is a multi-dimensional artist born and raised in Detroit, MI. Now residing
in Portland, OR, she is a Medicine Woman who heals herself and others through energy healing
and creative self-expression. She is the author of *Breaking Free.*

THE THING ABOUT MAKING YOUR BED ALONE

is that you're going to do it
over and over again
consciously or unconsciously
you will straighten all the creases
that have made themselves at home
for a while
you will re-center your sheets
once more
you will never know
what's the right side but it doesn't
matter, some days you still wake up
on the wrong side anyway
and look
you have a heater now
you feel warmer now
your hands
and feet no longer shiver at night
even when you're laid at a stranger's bed
even here, there's a home
for your body's too beautiful
not to be held
like this

MARJ OSTANI is a multi-hyphenate author of *Homecoming*, columnist of *Unmasking*, editor
of *Love Letters En Route* newsletter, and host of *Just Checking In* podcast. Born in Manila,
Philippines, they aim to increase and expand stories for artists of non-dominant identities.

THINGS THAT DON'T SUCK

after Andrea Gibson

My cat making biscuits on my stomach/ My cat stealing food off my plate/ My
cat/ Dogs/ Doing the crossword over coffee/ McDonald's French fries (except
when they do)/ Three-hour phone calls with friends who live in another state/
Star Wars movie marathons/ Sushi dates/ The smell of the pavement after
it rains/ Pedicures/ Flip-flops/ Singing Taylor Swift in the car/ Pumpkins/
Reading outside in the sun/ Reading on the couch under a blanket/ Bubble
baths/ Fuzzy socks/ Squirrels taking nuts from your hand/ Getting drunk off
margaritas/ Flirting/ Placing your hand on their thigh/ Forehead kisses/ Soft
cardigans/ Hot tea in silly mugs/ The way your body feels elastic after yoga/
Your succulents growing wildly on their floating shelf/ Life, often.

TAMMY SUBIA lives in Connecticut with a cat who might be part dog. She drinks a lot of
matcha and owns too many mugs. If she's not writing or reading, she's probably watching
Gilmore Girls.

GOBLIN MODE

Lockdown ended and everyone declared living cool again,
while I sat in the dark
feasting on my heart.
My unwashed laundry,
my neglected wrappers were excellent company,
thank you!

I fell asleep
with a plate that once held toast, one thumb hovering
over a stale google search that read *"gyms near me."*
The other fist in a family bag of crisps.
Begrudgingly wake just to sigh
at my surroundings and think,
yes, now I understand Tracey Emin's *My Bed.*

I played The Sims,
for 14 hours straight,
to practice small talk. I cut the fringe
with rusted nail scissors
to consider feeling.

are
you
still
watching?

I looked up one day and learned
I haven't moved in years.
I'd like to get moving again but
there are aches even lavender baths can't soothe.

Open screen I keep
the results of my personality test on hand
just in case
I forget who I am.

AIMEE SCANLON is a part-time poet living in Warwickshire, UK. She studied literature at university and found her way to the page after graduating. Her work focuses on mental health, class, and gender issues in modern Britain.

QUILTED THING

Did you know that our hearts are broken from the start?
Within minutes of our first breath,
a hole between the two chambers of our hearts should close.

Not for good though, right?

Not for forever.
Mine's been broken a hundred times.

By strangers on the street with lovely eyes
or maybe they were broken down aweary.

They've sung me songs
or played me a tune.
They've sidled up close
and made my eyes teary.

But proximity leads
those I love most
to break my heart most often
and with deft skill.

They can take me down
with a single word
or by withholding affection or attention.

Maybe hearts are made to be broken.

We busy ourselves
putting our energy
into plugging holes,

repairing our makeshift piece of machinery,
over and again.

We are a patched-up piece of work.
Stapled, sewn and glued together with spit and feathers.
Each patch a memory.

But,
as the memories lose their sting

we find
we've become a lovely quilted thing.

KAYLEIGH BRODEUR is a forty-something mom of three. This is her first foray into risking her heart and soul to be seen. Well, not exactly her first, but, it somehow feels riskier than marriage and children, something more akin to signing a mortgage.

SO YOU FOUND ME . . . ON INSTAGRAM.

And look! Am I the water that you wished for,
purified and vitamin enriched,
hallucinogenic and holographic?

Do the ripples of my river
glimmer with the rhythm in your ears:
a song, the wind, your deafening bedtime heartbeat?

Seek me out to try to escape yourself again.

Does my new love fold into the second dimension
in a way you can understand?
Can you understand?
Are you worried

that you never loved me well enough
to make my surface sparkle like you wanted,
like it does now, like something good and worthy,
like children laughing
in the park playground
on the steel slide
on the grass hill?

So you found me,
and was I what you were looking for?
Was I then? And am I now? No,
you can't admit what you want:
a flower, or a seed.
Your doctor might prescribe an album or the sun.
Maybe a clam or a worm.

One day you'll bite a thing,
and you'll become intolerant to all other foods.
Even water.

EILEEN WARD is an Irish-American poet from Long Beach, NY. with a BA from Villanova
University, where she pursued a concentration in writing and rhetoric. She founded the Villanova
Poetry Society and established the university's annual poetry slam.

THE PATRON SAINT OF STRAWBERRY LEMONADE & WEIRD EARRINGS

I practice self-love
like a fist cracking against drywall.
I have no knack for self compassion,
but I buy myself earrings shaped like
mushrooms and it feels close to
the same thing. I want to be as beautiful
as a doe lying sweetly in a flower field,
as functional as the bullet whizzing
through her eye. I want to feel so strong,
so sure, instead of petals in a hurricane
or gas station corndogs. I want to be so
soft, so good, but I'm eggshells crumpling
into cake batter. I split the sorrow from
my body and feel its absence like
a phantom limb. Self-love, it turns out,
is just Monday morning breakfast, just
clean teeth and bloody gums, but it feels
like a ten-car pile up, like crawling through
mirror shards. I practice good posture as if
I'm someone who knows a thing or two.
I practice self-forgiveness as if I'm something
gentle enough to be held in mother arms.
Semisweet, I wax more than I wane. I ripen
more than I rot..I pull depression from
the bags under my eyes and watch it slip
glittering down the drain. I hold myself like
a new lover, take all this self-love into my bone
marrow. I practice believing it'll stay inside me,
not seep out of my wounds. I practice hoping,
hoping, hoping, and it passes through my skin,
candescent as sunlight, full to the brim with
something I can't yet name.

WANDA DEGLANE is a poet and therapist from Arizona. She is the author of *Melancholia*
and other books of poetry. A writer from a young age and a poet since high school, she enjoys
lavender-flavored ice cream and snuggling with her orange cat, Nico.

THE MULTICOLORED SOUL

The mirror reflects an image unclear,
A face divided, neither there nor here,
A kaleidoscope of colors and hues,
A portrait of a person still confused.

The skin a canvas of tones so varied,
Like colors of the earth freshly quarried,
A patchwork of cultures and lands,
An identity that still eludes my hands.

Am I the melting pot of many,
A fusion of cultures that's not any,
Or am I a stranger to them all,
A person divided, destined to fall?

I search for answers in the stars above,
In the faces of people that I love,
In the roots that anchor me to the earth,
In the voices that may tell me my worth.

And yet, the mirror still reflects
A face unsure, a heart that expects,
A day when I will finally see
The beauty of the person that's truly me.

Until that day, I'll search and roam,
And find my place to call my own,
A place where I am understood,
A person of variety, a person of good.

J.C. JOHNSTON is a disabled woman in her twenties, raised in a multiracial, immigrant household. Her love for the outdoors – backpacking, cross-country camping, hiking – breathes life into her work, serving as a profound source of inspiration.

SHARKS

I wonder, what have I gained
from all this holding back?
Instead of just jumping into the sea
without a second thought, I wait —
listen to anxiety whisper in my ear,
tell me that the water is too cold,
that I could drown,
that there could be sharks.
And so (as always),
hesitation becomes refusal.
I cling to the safety of the sand
and watch the others enjoy
what the ocean has to give.
But then, a far more important question
rolls in with the waves,
and I wonder, what have I *lost*
from all this holding back?
It seems that all along,
the sharks were only in my mind.

SABINA LAURA is a writer, poet, and illustrator from the UK. She is the author of several
poetry collections: *Moonflower, All This Wild Hope, Shades of Sorrow, When I Fall, A Little
Sunshine and a Little Rain: A Poetry Journal,* and *Silver Linings.*

EMOCEAN

I'm convinced *emotion*
is just *ocean*
terribly misspelled

when we're ecstatic
we say it feels like we're floating
we hold our breath in anticipation
drown ourselves in sorrow
feel the weight of grief pool in our lungs
and when someone states something profound
we say *that's deep*

to feel blue is not to feel sad
it is to admit we are still kicking
still swimming
still painfully and joyously alive

MICHELLE ARMITAGE is a mother and poet from Lake Country, BC. When not cuddled up
with her kids, you will likely find her barefoot in the garden, trying new recipes in the kitchen, or
capturing the magic of everyday life through words and photographs.

PASSIN'

Tres-pass-in' on my soil
I'm pass-in' on your toil
Climbin' over barbs
Gunna find me arid oil
Gunna find me who is loyal
Be their brother, be their foil

Don't know where your cock crows
Don't know what nobody knows
You're in the throes you can't compose
you're gettin' in my face
with your polyphonic prose
I'm pass-in'

I'm passin'
going over those wires
going over those fires
gunna see the field;
the crop yield, the no big dealed,
what's not revealed, the sailor keeled
the preacher healed;
goldfield, minefield, oilfield, outfield,
which field is your battlefield?
Trespassin'?

Trespassin'
after passin' on the moon
the sealed heat shield peeled yield and kneeled
I'm passin'
move aside, and let that man go thru
I'm passin'
Trespassin'
a suited-up assassin, in burnin' Laos
I'm passin'

82

Trespassin'
a suited-up finance man, in my bank account
I'm passin'
Trespassin'
a suited up robot cop with the head count
I'm passin'
Trespassin'
on my grandpa's farm
find that fella who did you harm
the firearm that tripped the burglar alarm

but take a close look at that alarm
it is false;
you take a pause
there is no cause
there is peace, on my tone arm
feel the charm
for alarm
I'm pass-in'
Tres-pass-in'

E.M. TEICHMAN is an architect. On Sundays, when the firearms are silent, he wanders the hills of eastern Pennsylvania looking for poems.

ADAPTED

There's this point
when you've been in the darkness
for so long
that if you just hang on
if you keep going in that lightless space
eventually you'll begin
making your own flame
your eyes will adjust and you'll begin to see
that the cage you've felt hostage in
were trees on the edge of a forest
and just beyond them
your lantern
will illuminate the sky.

LOGAN MCRAE BLANTON is a writer, poet, mindset and health coach, traveler, and mental health advocate based in Seattle, WA. He is currently prepping the release of his debut novel and has other writings and musings that can be found on his website and social media platforms.

COME, SIT WITH ME

Come, sit with me.
I'll boil the kettle
and we'll have tea,
sip spearmint
and settle the waves
rolling in our stomachs.

Come,
tell me about your heartbreak
and I'll tell you how to stitch
the pieces back together.
I'll show you my scars
and whisper stories
while these slender fingers
leech warmth
from a china cup of bone.

I'll remind you of
heartstrings that snapped,
grew wild and restless,
climbed a mountain far too rough,
and slipped down the jagged rock face
when the wind blew in with malice.

Come,
I'll help you fill the emptiness
that's nestled inside your aching chest.
Let me refill your cup
so you might sip again a little too soon
and feel the fire that I know still burns
behind those lifeless eyes of yours.

Sit with me,
sweeten the spearmint
if you must,
and tell me of your heart,
and how it once loved too much.

SHELBY MARIE is a poet from Ontario, Canada. She is the author of the poetry collection *To Walk on Moonbeams*. Shelby loves antique things and everything that autumn brings. When she's not writing poetry, you'll often find her curled up with a book or journaling.

STILL HERE

There will be days
When hope's rays
Warmly envelop your soul
A solace of sunrise
Making it easy to feel whole

There will be days
When hope's light
Is hidden, out of sight
Tucked away behind
A cold dark blanket of moonlight.

But most days
Hope will rise on a heart slowly
Gentle and patient
Appearing so subtly
A dance on the breeze,
Bears witness to the
Hues and hymns
Of the changing leaves,
Planted firmly amongst the trees
To meet weary travelers
And offer reprieve
From the things the darkness has tried
To make them believe.

It speaks to our fear,
Hope gently glimmers
Like a slow burn it simmers,
Flickering faithfully it whispers:
"I'm still here. Still here."

LIZ NEWMAN is a poet and a writer from the Midwest who writes primarily on grief, faith, and mental health and is the author of *I Look to the Mourning Sky*. Her words have been shared in various publications, including in the London Underground.

CONTENTS

Thank you for supporting the first annual Central Avenue Poetry Prize, which showcases the talents of new and established poets. Each published poet has earned either a cash prize or an honorarium.

Look for the next edition in spring 2025.